FINISHING LINE PRESS

www.finishinglinepress.com

Thrive

poems by

Sarah Hirsch

Finishing Line Press
Georgetown, Kentucky

Thrive

ACKNOWLEDGMENTS

Thank you to *The Somerville Times* for publishing "To the woman" in *Off The
Shelf Press*, and to the *Country Dance and Song Society* for publishing "Orbit."

Publisher: Leah Huete de Maines
Editor: Christen Kincaid
Cover Art: Sarah Hirsch
Author Photo: Frank Kreimendahl
Cover Design: Elizabeth Maines McCleavy

Order online: www.finishinglinepress.com
            also available on amazon.com

Author inquiries and mail orders:
Finishing Line Press
PO Box 1626
Georgetown, Kentucky 40324
USA

Contents

*Dedicated to my mom, who taught me to read and garden
and swim and love freely,
and to my dad, who showed me a fierce strength,
always challenged me,
and could out-eat me in home grown hot pepper contests*

*Endless thanks to wonderful Max, who delights me, feeds me,
and lifts me up. I love you*

Hot

When I first ran my hands down the
valley of your chest,
they were rough and edged in soot

I had spent that week and the one before
in a smithy, pounding form into steel,
watching as the fire transformed

black rods into quietly glowing embers,
orange and pink at first, then yellow
with a growing audacity and heat of their own

and finally before the white hot sparking,
before the heat became too much
for the integrity of what is solid,

for metal too can burn—all things
catch fire—
strike

weld together the vines at their melting
for I was making vines, at the time
that I met you.

To grow

At school, we are planting seeds

zinnias sweet pea and
na-stur-tium (shum, na stur shum)

the children regard their jars of dirt
with the entire scope
of human experience: horror, enthralled,
curious, mischievous,
earnest

I watch as two boys pack in soil,
one intent on shoving as much as possible
mashing the soft peat, getting the most
and the other pinching each clod with a pinky up
grace and dropping it, somewhat unconvinced,
with soft, fragrant thuds

finger sized holes for each seed
and a gentle dirt blanket, nighty night
says a girl, and then water and what
else do plants need to grow
sun! sun, they need sun!

We lay synchronized

like holes like
air, we were nestled
against vertebrae, smooth
brush against my
face blush
hot
in your sound
and the care
free throw of your
arm, like it didn't matter
that I could
bend the delicate
hairs like golden bows like
bridges like sunshine
and blow them over

just with a breath

Bodysurfing

You have to throw yourself
face
down
right as the power of the wave is surging around your thighs

inhale and hold it, arms up in a leap water streaming
and let it take you

pulling and tumbling over
a roaring

God (maybe) and Cancer

Maybe it's on the surgeon's table but
I think it's earlier, in the waiting room

a bellywave of faith perhaps or is it
compassion or is it

acceptance (the hush sadness of bowed heads
a cancer waiting room at 7:30 am,

everyone just... waiting
Can you help me will I live)

or perhaps this is hope

Uncomfortably, I'll admit
there's a subconscious pride (or lying?)

(or perhaps all pride is lying)
that comes with never having been cut

open
before this, of course. Now it's

obvious, grotesque, that it was only ever luck
Flamboyance of health

Is this faith? Allowing, begging this woman
to reach in when all my body rebels

Trusting skill, science, hope
that this will heal

A List of My Mother's Lovers

A list of my mother's lovers; if we can't fix the world just try, try to
make any one thing more beautiful; a revery on politics and justice

She told me, I had to wear a plaid skirt to elementary school
and got sent home the day my growth spurt dangled my knees
tantalizingly below the hem, whore girl, and I walked along the road
knee socks not quite masking the female body that was made
to torment men

when I was fourteen, she said, I fell in love with a boy
with sandy hair and an apologetic manner, glasses, the works
we exchanged crumpled notes, sweet nothings in secret code
and eventually, made out behind the pines, off the path
winding from the cranberry bogs

at sixteen, though, there was someone else, and she grew quiet, so
childhood me dug out that old yearbook and there he is, smirking
his sexual consciousness circled in a red pen accompanied by,
Hey Barb, it was great
getting to know you

her parents slept in separate twin beds, and indulged in sin
twice monthly, I imagine, and came down hard on her
curls were immodest, boys were the devil and soon
she had quit school and moved to Boston

as a bisexual loading dock worker
she told me, my roommate was a night club dancer and I loved
watching her move and we didn't have a refrigerator but we
fought like we cared in those snow filled streets and when
Calvin came along everything
changed

he brought her to his Alabama family, Black and
didn't the world stare, she said he taught her to cook,
and canoe, and they wanted to have a baby, but
he was drafted, and years later came back,
changed

and she wanted a child
and a home and somehow,
she said, the long and winding
found her way
to me

Freckles

Sun spangles cluster on the rounded cusps
of my shoulders, nose, ears
constellations, heat maps

these are badges of time in the light,
days graced
and golden

tribute to the hours
of meandering conversation
hands waving, drawing,

coming to rest,
calloused memories and skill
gently exploring

feet dangling off the dock
into jade water, bobbing up with cool
swells

as shadows purple and birds
change their calls
to evensong.

When I was five, I stood on the bathroom sink
and glared at mirror me,
so unrepentantly spotty

so I pierced the skin of my face
with my nails,
trying to pry off

every
last
spot

they've only spread since then and now
I don't so much mind the miracle
of summer warmth

Awake

When you dream
of someone lost,
warm touch and
that voice
encompassing—
how do you wake?

Thrive

Maybe it's the still blueness
this morning, or the lilies
planted so long ago bursting
stardust pollen fireworks everywhere
defiant orange joy

or remembered summers and
wet cool grass imprinting on the
smalls of our backs as we stare up
up in darkness and watch for the slight dance
of starlight and talk of anything but
death and maybe it's that I've grown, some

or maybe it's the shoreless ripples of someone else's
disaster, and what will become of these stories
another thread in the core of me wrapped
tight in a spiral down around all those
sun hot garden days with my mother
our backs curved carefully over the
question of what will live
and thrive

An early thaw

A soft day like this
is sometimes how I wind up
in trouble

when the sap runs snow melts tight new buds burst
even if
it's only for today

there's this excitement I can't fully explain,
my whole body remembers
what it's like to be immersed in green salt water

limbs and face and chest bare
the air gentle
and so alive

electric hands at the start of a dance, pulled together
from across the spinning room
tumult, full of beautiful distractions

the sudden panache of an old friend
reappearing to say hello
history unembarrassed of goodbyes

Predawn symphony

His bare back flows up dappled
in the play of streetlight and
curtain and leafy vine

familiar hands move silently
not to wake me,
tugging down stiff fabric

wrapping his torso,
deepening shadow
outside, the biggest sky, tips

open like a spilled bowl
shot through with watercolors,
seeping orange into blue

Harbinger

The peepers are calling tonight and
sometimes I get so caught up in
what has happened and
might

that it takes the song of some yearning
wild thing,
reverberating

from one spring to
the next
or from the last, or even before that,

a long echo of memory
and
anticipation

I know your geometries

I know your geometries your
angularities the

division of power between
your arms and those thighs

the strength of sloping shoulders
and too well that fulcrum

the about which
we turn, negative space

where everything
hangs in the balance

Orbit

You can feel that
pull,
momentum

an arc of
someone's life

swung for a moment
into you
eyes locked

and there's a certain
embarrassment

a caught me gasp
but there's no time
for we have already seen each other

as we move through sound
each of us a particular story,

a satellite of yearning and touch
distance and
realization of love, maybe

I can only believe love
knows many forms

before we tessellate and
realign and know
someone else

again

New

He's curled with his ribcage sobbing heavy
on his knees, small
shaking body so sad
and so angry at
something
an ephemera, maybe
passing comment or
disappointment
but nonetheless, so real
so world tilting and
desperate
that all is given up
in a wail

sometimes it's comical
we the grown the fossilized
the experienced, with our
baggage
of perspective
we know it's not
a big deal

but I wonder at staying close
to that intensity
of laughter at any joke, because
all of them are new

forgiveness in the next breath
because you
can't remember
a hurt that
lasted

To the Woman

To the woman with the pendulating breasts:
Thank you.

Stony expression fixed on the blinking walk signal
flashing bright against the wash of post-deluge dawn,
a weathered, strong knuckle grip anchored to a cardboard coffee cup

faded baseball cap shoved tight over tin hair
metal-stubborn curling out sideways in a relentless fight for flight
bouncing slightly with each step

as your breasts swing free, long with the care
of children, almost certainly, and lovers,
gravity and age lived

the thin cotton of your top a
tenuous barrier against the heat
of July and gaze of strangers.

Thank you, because I dreamt of my mother and woke up
missing her, and wishing
I could see her solidly
marching along a sidewalk, bra-less and brazen.

Oh, I'm fine

You mustn't wear your tragedy
like a t-shirt, so casually thrown on
a stain too aching for the everyday

nevertheless the light
may shine through sometimes

watery eyes, a sharp gasp

in the softest moments
or a firm touch

jostled on the train, clanging
lost in all the metal scope of humanity

you may see something of her
in his face

and find yourself suddenly weeping

wrapped in the arms of someone
who guesses perhaps
at the deep water just beyond

Rainbow

I like to keep a prism on the window sill
for those early morning hints of sun
low angled winter-bright and bare,
gray cold truth itself

and then I'll move about not thinking, and suddenly
spangled

I am a radiance of color

I remember
saturation, vibrance
the possible

Underpinnings

There's something about
the dull smack of a hand hitting wood
and the staggering fall of drunken weight

something about the shape of those words
so cutting and ugly and loud, the animal wail
released when glass shatters on the floor

something about the blood throbbing in my temples
as I ease my child's body along the purple black shadow
hugged close to the wall as in spy games, but so not

not anything I'd wish on anyone, safe now in my own
home my own bed my own lover my own now
but when the upstairs neighbors start shouting and

something falls, they holler as it
bounces once, twice
and clatters still into sickening silence

Things we don't talk about

Things we don't talk about, part 5: age 8 or so, watching my mom as
she, drunk, prepares to hurl herself into the sea, again

Delirious and gone from here, yet righteously enraged by things that
     are true
she tears away like a wind released, down the potholed street
knees high, bursting through the towel she has thrown over her
     bathing suit
out of force of habit, I guess, for when you go to commit suicide you
     don't
need to dry off

I am chasing her, wailing, desperate, uselessly small
we live just uphill from the beach, a beautiful ribbon of sand
that steely waves curl onto, again and again, rounding the stones
and sucking them back out, dragging them down across the chasm
too turbulent to follow, in our soft buoyant human bodies

We continue on that way, she in the lead, in a way, both hysterically
     crying
putting on a show for the island neighbors who know all our woes
and look away, because it is a small community and really, it's
embarrassing, the way they carry on like this, in our streets,
and we get as far as the cusp of the waves

They thunder gray and green, november might and majesty.
It is cold, and sometime in the uncanny evening hours—no one
else is tempted, drawn to the danger, intoxicating pull of the salt water
the human craven need for sheer scale dulled by other wants of
comfort, platitudes, walls and stability and trust

She is standing there in water swirling up to her thighs, towel
     discarded
now, crumpled on the shore and I, I go to stand by it, to pick it up and
     shake off

the sand, instincts preserving habit in this act of what could be,
    this time,
ultimate destruction, I know, of a life so tortured, so full up of joy
    and love and yet
unbearable in its pain and abuse and limits

She turns around, and sees me, really sees me for the first time
    that night
as the water washes against her legs, cold and sobering, not
    unlike
the saline flowing within our own bodies, surging with tides and
delicious with the tiniest of creatures and unknowable things.
Not today. She comes step by step out of the waves, collapses into the
    dry towel.

2 a.m. in the ER, my father's third stroke

The harsh lights of the hospital pulse
flash, nauseate me

watching the man next cot over
bleed out from four bullet wounds

would giving him human grace be
to look away, or to bear witness?

I rivet my eyes on you, seeing your
massive body as a bird wrapped in tissue

struggling feeble strength required to raise
just one finger

on the paralyzed side of the body
that is half of you

that just stopped functioning
half a 250 pound man of anger, muscle, brain

so powerful, often so
terrible

but how can I
when you're lying there, unable to swallow

I can't lose
you both

An orchestra of spaces

Raise your arms
and open

your mouth
stop.

Let air fill
you

chill the insides
of your cheeks.

Let all thrumming

of city faces touch words
warming flashing

pulsing and beating
within the solidity of you

become an
orchestra

of spaces, of winter.

Edges

I think it's on these days that I let myself
feel the edges
where you were

I have dreams where we're walking, together
along the beach usually, all wind and light
and the rushing of the sparkling water

they're very normal dreams
in which nothing much happens
except that you're here

like a punch—the ache in that—
the dissolve upon waking and the weight of now—
gone

it's these edges that I can't always keep
my eye on,
too sad, too keening for the everyday

because we do keep going, don't we
that's the joy and the greatest triumph and
maybe, the biggest sadness

this mingled growth and loss and
memory, a fractured sense
a yearning to ask you

what you might think
of the parts of me that are you
but without
you

When you must start again

When you must start again
(and we must)

it can be good to start small

grasp only what you can hold
perhaps in one hand

so that the other is free

to catch, to
rest

against your head as light
pressure

remember to breathe

perhaps
hold it with both hands anyway

carefully cradled

like an echo, a repeated chance

Now I Am Not a Sunrise Girl

Now I am not
a sunrise girl by nature

Dark warmth of bed
pulls heavy on my limbs and
turns my chin back,

back to dreams, as real as
day, breathing into the shoreline
of my lover's ribcage

a rhythm of moving gently forward,
continuing,
in step

and a tidal force of
whatever I am already doing
familiar, beloved, the

five more minutes
seducing comfort before
change

is usually enough to condemn an early rising

but I looked up and a pink curl
of cloud catapulted off a
neighbor's roof

and as I watched, the sun spilled
into the open rafters
of an attic under construction

filling the dark purples with gold and
crisp, certain
shape

It is a time of great change

Yesterday evening I sat on porch steps
sun humming the pink oranges
of a day well dissolved down
past the peaked rooftops and fingerbone trees.
A mellowing, a warming.

It is a time of great change

my friend says. She believes
as the planets form a square, lives shift,
drawn to each other. Upheaval of the damp earth
by seeds pushing green, demanding to the sky, unfurling
one then two cotyledon leaves, rubber fresh, is only just the start.

A couple, in step, walking up the sidewalk are drawn to my lap
by their old dog, who places his head on my knees, Love me
he says, for we are alive, and it is a time of great change.
His ears are soft and graying fur in my hands loosens, explodes
in great clouds of scatterplot dandelion wish drifts

The man tells us a story of his mother, a strong
Greek woman who once, in a pinch,
dragged his four siblings and luggage tied to a rope
through customs to find America, but
first, god help us, a restroom

And the woman, his wife maybe, laughs
but only looks down at the dog, his panting head heavy
against my touch
She's told me that story, your mom,
pinched my arm and said, You're not as strong as me.

The sky deepens to a richness a royalty
color for ballgowns, resplendent, swimmable.
The cement stoop remembers heat, radiating
up through my thighs, my chilled fingers
nails showing light purple.

It is a time of great change.

With Thanks

So many thanks to Max, Ben, Molly, Stephen, Jeff, Brendan, Vivian, Cecile, Rachel, Allie, Oscar, Jenny, Jordan, Cailin, Rebecca, Adrian, and Cedric. All those years of giving me support and kindness and feedback and edits and encouragement—thank you, sincerely. Thank you. It's all meant more than you may know.

Thank you so much to Finishing Line Press and their very patient and encouraging team, my editor Christen Kincaid, and to those I may never meet who took the chance reading my most personal, most vulnerable stories, and helped usher them into print.

Sarah Hirsch is a painter, writer, and teacher. She lives by the sea in Rhode Island with her partner and their oodles of critters, and she loves to open water swim, garden, fiddle, sing, and contra dance, and organizes community folk events. Sarah holds a Master's of Education from Lesley University, Montessori teacher certification, a B.A. from Colby College, and received a Fulbright grant to teach in Morocco. After the first professional decade focused on teaching and administration, she transitioned to freelance. Her award-winning oil paintings have been shown across the region (and occasionally in other countries) and she has written and illustrated a few children's books, with more in progress. Her poetry has appeared in several area publications. This is her first poetry chapbook. Her work can be followed online at *www.sghirsch.com*